THE FIRST EXPLORERS IN
SPACE

by

rge

a Capstone company — publishers for children

Engage Literacy is published in the UK by Raintree.
Raintree is an imprint of Capstone Global Library Limited, a company incorporated in England and Wales
having its registered office at 264 Banbury Road, Oxford, OX2 7DY – Registered company number:
6695582

www.raintree.co.uk

Editorial credits
Erika L. Shores, editor; Peggie Carley and Cynthia Della-Rovere, designers; Tracy Cummins,
media researcher; Katy LaVigne, production specialist

Image credits
Alamy: ITAR-TASS Photo Agency, 13; Dreamstime: Oscarharaldsson, Cover Left; Getty Images: Express
Newspapers, 23, Keystone-France, 12, Science & Society Picture Library, 18-19; NASA: Johnson Space
Center: Cover Right, Cover Middle, 1, 16-17, 21 Top, 21 Bottom, 24, 27, 28-29; NASA: KSC, 3, 20;
Newscom: Fine Art Images Heritage Images, 15, Ogonyok/ZUMAPRESS, 14, TASS/ZUMA Press, 7;
Science Source: Detlev van Ravenswaay, 10, RIA Novosti, 9; Shutterstock: Everett Historical, 22, Graphic
Compressor, 6, SergeyDV, Cover Back, 30, Triff, Design Element, xtock, 5

21 20 19 18 17
10 9 8 7 6 5 4 3 2 1
Printed and bound in China.

The First Explorers in Space

ISBN: 978 1 4747 4706 6

Text note: Names of spacecraft are considered titles and are placed in italics, just like book titles.

CONTENTS

WHAT IS SPACE?

People dreamed of going into space for many years. Because space is nothing like Earth, it's hard to explore.

Space is the area outside Earth's *atmosphere*, the thin layer of gases around our planet. One of the gases is *oxygen*. People and animals need it to breathe. In space, there is very little oxygen.

Things float in space because there is less *gravity* than on Earth. Gravity is what pulls objects towards each other. It's what keeps you on the ground.

The first brave space explorers had to find ways to travel into space and deal with low gravity. They needed spacesuits and a way to breathe.

Everything beyond Earth's atmosphere is called space.

First person to orbit Earth

Space travel started with a *satellite* called *Sputnik 1*. It was the first machine to go beyond Earth's atmosphere. *Sputnik 1* was *launched*, or sent into space, by the Soviet Union on 4 October, 1957. This country is now Russia. *Sputnik 1* *orbited*, or went around, the planet. It stayed in space for three months before burning up as it fell back to Earth.

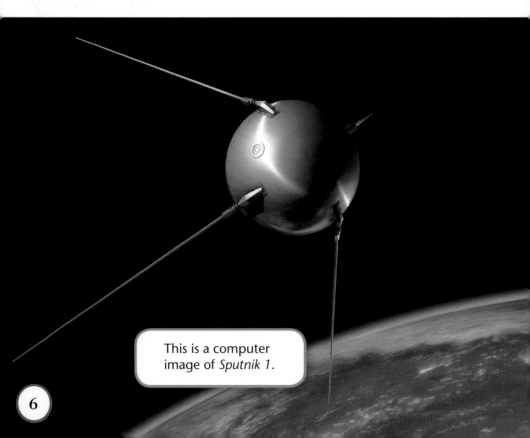

This is a computer image of *Sputnik 1*.

Yuri Gagarin was the
first person in space.

In 1961, the Soviets sent
the first person into space.
Yuri Gagarin flew once around
Earth on 12 April, 1961. It
took 1 hour and 48 minutes.

During the quick flight, Yuri said that his pencil and paper floated in the air because of low gravity. Yuri also ate meat out of a tube like toothpaste. He did this to show that you could eat in space.

Yuri was the first person to ever look down from space. He saw Earth like a big blue marble below. He saw clouds from above and said it was very beautiful.

Yuri getting ready for his flight into space.

Yuri and parachute

Yuri's spacecraft and parachute returning to Earth

Yuri's spacecraft dropped back to Earth on its own at the end of the flight. The outside parachute opened. This large piece of cloth filled with air and slowed down the spacecraft. Yuri burst out of the spacecraft in his seat. Then his own parachute opened. He sailed down until he landed in a field near a small town in the western Soviet Union. Yuri went to a nearby camp. He had to use the phone to say where he had landed.

First woman in space

About two years later, the Soviets sent the first woman into space. Valentina Tereshkova was skilled at jumping out of planes using a parachute. Because of this, she was chosen as one of four women to travel in space. She trained for a year. She blasted off in *Vostok 6* on 16 June, 1963, and spent nearly three days orbiting Earth. She went around Earth 48 times.

Valentina Tereshkova was the first woman to travel into space.

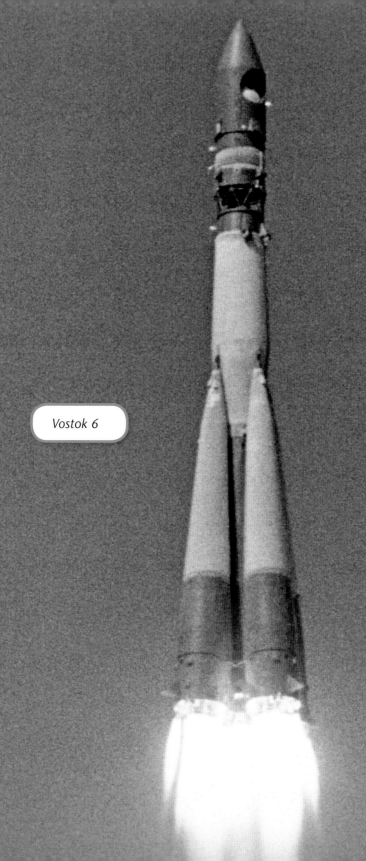

Vostok 6

Valentina inside *Vostok 6*

During her flight Valentina took pictures from space. She also spoke by radio with the pilot of another Soviet spacecraft, *Vostok 5*. It was going around Earth at the same time. When she returned, Valentina was called a hero in the Soviet Union.

FIRST DOG IN SPACE

Before sending the first person into space, the Soviets sent up the first animal. *Sputnik 2* launched on 3 November, 1957. It held a small dog called Laika, or "barker".

Laika lay on a soft bed with straps to hold her in place. She had bowls with food and water. Cameras inside *Sputnik 2* sent back pictures of Laika eating.

Sadly, a return trip home had not been planned. Laika died after a few hours in space. But the dog's flight showed people that animals could survive a space launch.

First person on the Moon

The Soviet space programme was doing very well. The United States wanted to catch up! *NASA* had been working on spaceflight since 1958. NASA is a group of people based in the United States who work to learn about space and space travel. After watching the Soviets put a man in orbit, NASA wanted to do more than just fly in space.

Neil Armstrong

They wanted to put the first person on the Moon. *Apollo 11* was launched on 16 July, 1969, with three people on board who were called *astronauts*. They were Neil Armstrong, Buzz Aldrin and Michael Collins.

Michael Collins

Buzz Aldrin

Columbia

The *Apollo 11* spacecraft had two parts. The main part was called *Columbia*. The part made to land on the Moon was called *Eagle*.

On 20 July, 1969, Collins let *Eagle* go from the main part of the spacecraft. Collins circled in space above the Moon. Armstrong and Aldrin flew *Eagle* to the Moon's surface. It took two hours. When they arrived, Armstrong said that the *Eagle* had landed.

Eagle

Armstrong and Aldrin put on spacesuits that had backpacks with oxygen. Armstrong opened *Eagle's* door and climbed down a short ladder. He then opened a case on the outside of *Eagle* that held a TV camera. Millions of people on Earth watched Armstrong step onto the Moon.

Armstrong and Aldrin took photos and did tests on the Moon for two and a half hours. They gathered soil and rocks from the Moon. They even left behind a sign. It had the date of their landing and said they came in peace from planet Earth.

Aldrin stands next to the US flag on the Moon.

Armstrong and Aldrin left behind this sign on the Moon.

HERE MEN FROM THE PLANET EARTH
FIRST SET FOOT UPON THE MOON
JULY 1969, A.D.
WE CAME IN PEACE FOR ALL MANKIND

Columbia was the first shuttle launched by NASA. It flew into space on 12 April 1981.

FIRST AMERICAN WOMAN IN SPACE

A few years after *Apollo 11*'s flight, NASA stopped sending people to the Moon. Instead they sent *shuttles* into space. Shuttles were early flying science labs. Astronauts lived and worked on board for weeks. They did tests in space.

NASA began looking for women and people of other races to work in space. In January 1977, student Sally Ride saw a story in her university newspaper. It said NASA wanted to recruit women. Sally wrote to NASA and asked for a job.

Sally Ride was still at university when she applied to be an astronaut for NASA.

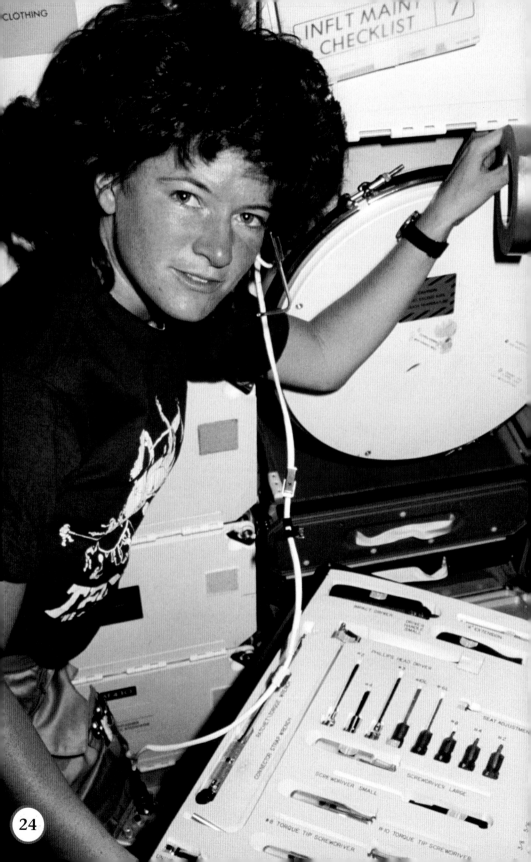

Sally was studying science and space at university. She also knew a lot about maths. NASA asked Sally to come and talk to them. In January 1978 she joined the astronaut programme and began training to travel into space.

Sally became the first US woman in space on 18 June, 1983, when she flew on the *STS-7 Challenger* shuttle. Part of Sally's job on the shuttle was using a robot arm to send a satellite into space. Sally called her work the most fun she'd ever had.

Sally holding tools on board the *Challenger* shuttle.

First African-American in space

The shuttle *Challenger's* next flight was a first for the history books, too. Guion Bluford, known as Guy, became the first African-American in space.

Guy had been a US Air Force pilot before joining NASA in August 1979. His first space flight was on the *STS-8 Challenger* on 30 August, 1983. Guy's mission was the first shuttle trip to both launch and land at night.

Guy Bluford was 41 years old when he flew on his first shuttle mission in 1983.

Later, Guy flew on a *Spacelab* mission in 1985. Spacelabs were special labs on board a space shuttle. NASA often shared Spacelab missions with other countries.

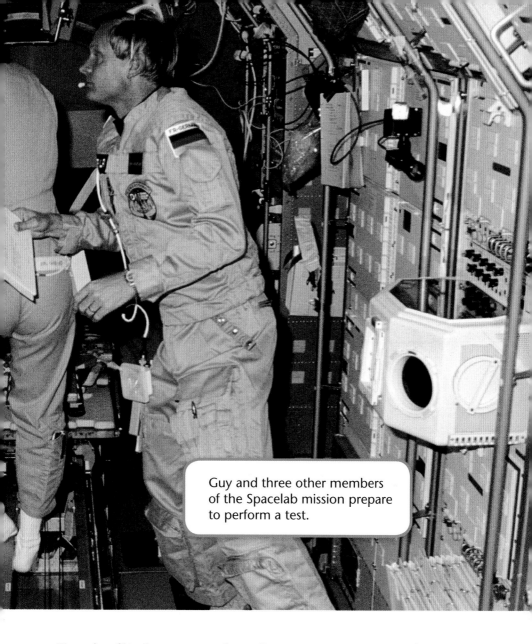

Guy and three other members of the Spacelab mission prepare to perform a test.

Guy's flight was the first to carry eight people into orbit. He and the rest of the crew performed 76 tests on board. Guy made a total of four trips into space and spent 688 hours of his life there.

WHAT'S NEXT TO EXPLORE?

Brave space explorers helped us learn more about what is beyond Earth. They tried out ideas, did tests and walked on the Moon. Much of what we know about space is because of them.

We still have much to discover about space. Today people continue to study and explore space. One day new space travel may include landing on other planets, such as Mars. To find out the secrets of Mars, other planets and beyond, we'll need many more bold explorers.

This image shows what a trip to Mars might look like in the future.

Glossary

astronaut person who is trained to live and work in space

atmosphere mixture of gases that surround Earth

gravity force that pulls objects together

launch send a rocket or spacecraft into space

NASA US government agency that does research on space exploration and flight; NASA stands for National Aeronautics and Space Administration

orbited travelled around an object in space

oxygen colourless gas that people and animals breathe

satellite spacecraft that circles Earth

shuttle spacecraft NASA used to send astronauts into space from 1981 to 2011

Spacelab special laboratory on board a space shuttle where astronauts perform experiments

Index